CAREERS IN

DIGITAL
JOURNALISM

REPORTING, CREATING, AND EDITING FOR THE NEW MEDIA

ONE OF THE MOST EXCITING NEW CAREERS today is the field of digital journalism. This new breed of professional reporter creates content for online news sites that are accessed through computers and apps on mobile devices. Some digital journalists work for traditional news outlets such as newspapers and television broadcasters, developing new reports or repurposing existing print news stories for online media. Others work for news sites that only exist in cyber space. Some are employed by news aggregation sites, gathering and organizing existing content from across the World Wide Web and presenting the news in a centralized location.

Digital journalism combines the writing and editing talents of traditional reporters with the multimedia skills of video photographers and editors, website designers and social media mavens. Digital journalists gather information and create highly visual, interactive news stories that are read and viewed by the general public, and increasingly by subscribers or members of a particular web service. They work with editors and visual creatives to mold their stories into engaging content that relates the facts and voices opinions in an innovative, entertaining fashion to keep visitors returning to the site.

Would you make a good digital journalist? Certainly technical training is required, both as a journalist and as an online content creator. Personal trails are also important for success. Are you a clear, concise writer who enjoys the creative process? Do you like solving puzzles – the challenge of digging out the answers to important questions that the people need to know? Are you adept with technology and open to learning new skills in a rapidly-evolving field? Do you have good organizational skills? Do you communicate well in person – a must for interviewing other people and when talking in front of a video camera? Do you like exploring the virtual online world and using mobile devices? If these characteristics sound like you, you may be well positioned to pursue a digital journalism career.

A four-year degree is generally required to start a career as a digital journalist. Many begin with degrees in journalism or communications, but some employers are more interested in technical savvy, digital creativity and multimedia storytelling skills. Graduate degrees are typically only required for management and high-ranking editorial positions, although many progress into leadership positions without additional formal education.

Digital journalists may work for native online news sites; or they may be employed by traditional newspapers, magazines, and TV and radio stations. Some of the latter groups write for both the print outlet and the website, while others create only digital content. Most of these digital journalists are employees of a single publication or website, while others are freelancers – independent journalists who write for a number of outlets on an as-needed basis.

The modern news cycle runs 24/7/365, so digital journalists can sometimes work around the clock, covering breaking news or traveling from one assignment to the next.

If you have good analytical, interpersonal, and technical skills, you can enjoy a rewarding career as a digital journalist. The right balance of training, hard work and appealing personal traits can help you achieve the personal and professional satisfaction of a successful digital journalist.

WHAT YOU CAN DO NOW

EVEN WHILE YOU ARE STILL IN HIGH school, you can begin laying the foundation for an intriguing career in digital journalism. Online media demand traditional reporting skills plus a working knowledge of technology and visual storytelling. The more English courses you can take, the better prepared you will be. Volunteering for your high school newspaper, starting a blog, editing your own videos and building social media networks will give you experience writing for different media. Start building a library of samples to add to your portfolio.

In addition to writing and editing skills, technology is critical in digital journalism. Classes on word processing software, computer graphics, web construction and design, videography, and desktop publishing tools will all be useful. If you are unable to find the right classes at your high school, investigate courses offered by local colleges and private schools. Online tutorials are a great way to learn about cutting-edge technology while it is still new.

Begin following practices used by professionals who are already employed in digital journalism. Read publications, watch podcasts, subscribe to blogs, attend speeches by journalists, and follow industry leaders on social media. Read industry periodicals (online and print). Visit professional association websites to stay up-to-date with industry trends. Attend local chapter meetings of professional journalists' groups, and inquire about student memberships. Many of these groups offer scholarships, volunteer opportunities, and match interns with employers. Getting involved in a professional association can help you improve your chances to find opportunities to jump-start your education and your career.

HISTORY OF THE PROFESSION

ROOTS OF TRADITIONAL JOURNALISM date back to the first periodical published in 1594. Newspapers soon followed in England, with the first American paper established in 1690 in Boston. By the 1770s, there were 89 newspapers published in 35 cities among the 13 American Colonies. By the early 1800s, publications evolved away from their alignment with political parties into privately owned businesses headed by independent editorial staffs. The New York Sun was the first "penny paper," selling for one cent per copy in 1833 and making news affordable to the general public. The New York Tribune, established in 1841, was the first paper with a national footprint. The Civil War in the 1860s had a major impact on newspapers and news magazines, with new technology such as the telegraph and photography allowing correspondents to report from the battlefields in words and pictures. Urban newspapers pooled their resources for better battlefield coverage, leading to news services like today's Associated Press and the first agencies attempting to gather news globally.

By 1914, the number of newspapers in the United States peaked at 14,000 weeklies and 2,600 dailies. Daily newspapers remained the dominant current information source for much of the 20th century, but new technologies brought more competition – from national radio networks in the 1920s, movie house newsreels in the 1930s, and colorful magazine photojournalism during World War II. By the 1950s, television networks combined the immediacy of radio with the realistic moving images of film, to create an even more compelling medium for reporting news. The full power of TV news became evident in the 1960s and 1970s as networks televised vivid images of the Vietnam War. The political and civil unrest of the 1960s also sparked "underground" and alternative newspapers that offered differing views of social issues than mainstream media provided – a trend later embraced by digital journalists.

Digital journalism did not upend the "traditional" news outlets of television, radio and print until the early 21st century. Digital journalism had been introduced in Great Britain in 1970 through the "teletext" system, which allowed subscribers to access brief, up-to-the-minute news articles. In 1979, Prestel introduced the Videotex system, which provided online versions of articles from major British newspapers. Computer hobbyists soon began using bulletin board systems (BBS) to communicate information among users, but like the other systems, BBS only had limited availability to the general public.

The first professional news site began in the early 1990s when The News & Observer newspaper in Raleigh, North Carolina, launched NandO Land (later shortened to "Nando"). However, the major factor in the explosion of online news was the introduction of the first commercial web browsers, Netscape Navigator in 1994 and Internet Explorer in 1995. Browsers and search engines helped power the proliferation of personal computers around the world, driving new demand for breaking news as it happened. By 1996, most major news organizations – already under pressure from round-the-clock cable television networks like CNN – launched their own news websites to keep pace with consumer expectations. News aggregators such as Yahoo!, America Online (now AOL) and Google, brought together news from different sites, allowing users to customize their news access through the World Wide Web.

Many of those early online news sources simply recycled articles and broadcast stories taken from newspapers, magazines, radio and TV. New media outlets soon emerged that provided original web-only news content. Salon, founded in 1995, was one of the first Internet-only news sites. Another influential outlet was The Drudge Report, which began as an email newsletter in 1996 and broke several national stories picked up by the major media. The number of online news sources increased rapidly, with digital publishers able to target niche audiences that mass media often ignored. Many sites provided exclusive content free of charge. These new outlets combined not only traditional print-style journalism, but also interactive graphics, video clips, hyperlinks to related news stories, and other features that newspapers and magazines could not duplicate. Blogs also opened the door to "citizen journalism," where anyone with a computer can post news and opinions online and find an audience. By 2008, more Americans got their national and international news from online sources than through newspapers.

The combination of new technology and financial pressures on traditional media further accelerated the rise of digital media. Online news outlets accessible by personal computers and mobile devices lured away former newspaper and magazine subscribers with free news, classified ads, interactive advertising, social media and other easy-to-personalize features. The loss of readers and viewers to the Internet – coupled with recessions in 2000 and 2008 – undercut the advertising revenues and business models that had supported newspapers, magazines, radio and television. A number of publications folded, went into bankruptcy, or slashed their staff in order to survive. While newspapers will survive for the foreseeable future, there are fewer general interest publications, fewer pages being printed in newspapers and magazines, and fewer employment opportunities in traditional media.

Publishers continue to seek a successful financial model to compete against "New Media" but thus far have had limited success. At the same time, the new landscape has opened up a world of opportunities for journalists, bloggers, and reporters to contribute content to a growing number of digital journalism outlets.

WHERE YOU WILL WORK

MANY DIGITAL JOURNALISTS WORK FOR the online sites of traditional news organizations, such as newspapers, magazines, newsletters, and radio and television broadcasters. Others work for "native" digital news outlets – organizations that provide news only through online sites accessed through personal computers and mobile devices.

These journalists may work for large national newspaper chains, mass media broadcast networks, or global interactive sites. Or they may write locally for small weekly or daily papers, local TV and radio stations, or a "hyper-local" online outlet like Patch.com or Examiner.com.

Competition is tough for jobs at nationwide outlets and major metropolitan publications. Traditionally, most journalists started out at smaller local papers, magazines, or stations, and then worked their way up to larger media markets over their careers. However, many digital journalists today start out at online publications that have a global readership, as many native digital news outlets prefer to hire young people straight out of college who bring the latest technical skills and a "digital attitude" to the job.

Today, almost half of all news analysts, reporters and correspondents work for newspaper, periodical, book and directory publishers. Another 20 percent of these journalists work for television broadcast companies and fewer than 10 percent are in radio.

Almost 10 percent have a more technical orientation,

working for data processing, web hosting and other information services. According to the Pew Research Center, fewer than half of the 5,000-plus digital journalists work for small online sites, while about 3,000 work for the largest 30 native news sites (including Huffington Post, Vice Media, Politico, BuzzFeed, Bleacher Report, Gawker, Mashable and Business Insider).

Journalism jobs have historically been concentrated in the major markets, such as New York, Los Angeles, Chicago, and Washington, DC. That trend remains true for digital journalists creating content for the online sites of large media companies, as well as some of the larger native digital news sites. However, the Internet also allows media companies and digital journalists to work in cities of all sizes – virtually anywhere they can connect with the Internet. Many digital journalists are able to work from home, on the road, or almost anywhere they like, only making occasional trips to larger cities to meet with the editorial staff or the subject of an interview.

Some digital journalists spend much of their time in the field, interviewing sources, covering breaking news or attending meetings. These reporters often travel to wherever news is happening and file their stories directly from that remote location. However, those who work for news aggregation services do not originate the content, but operate instead as curators and editors. They review content others create in print and on the web, collect stories for specific audiences (such as politics or fashion, or events in a particular location), summarize those articles, and provide links to the original sources. Other digital journalists spend time in an office or studio collaborating with video editors, audio technicians, and web masters as they weave words, pictures and sounds together to create multimedia presentations.

Most digital journalists are employed by a single digital site, although some work as freelancers. The independent journalists write articles for a variety of publications. They may be paid by the word, by the story, or by a monthly retainer tied to producing a certain number of posts or articles. Freelancers may also be stringers who have an ongoing relationship with several news organizations, contributing news from their geographic region or their assigned "beat" (area of specialization).

THE WORK YOU WILL DO

DIGITAL JOURNALISTS GATHER information from which they prepare online news presentations. This content may include the written word, video and audio segments, and other types of multimedia presentations. Some function like traditional journalists: conducting research, interviewing sources, attending meetings, and traveling to the scene of breaking news (such as a presidential debate or a Hollywood premiere). They supplement their words with photographs, and video and audio clips, gathered either by the journalist or by other creative professionals. They assemble the facts and audio-visual recordings to create a report. This report may be published as a print and/or web-based article; aired as a TV or radio newscast; or distributed as a multimedia presentation accessible by computers, smartphones and tablets. They may also broadcast their reports live over traditional stations and networks, and stream the events via the Internet.

Digital journalists work for a variety of organizations. Many are employed by traditional media outlets: newspapers, magazines, trade journals, newsletters, and television and radio stations. Others work for companies that produce their own publications, such as industry associations, trade unions, colleges and universities, nonprofits, hospitals, and private and public corporations. A significant number produce content for native online news sites, writing articles, editing videos and assembling news from across the Internet into a central location for easy viewing by their readers, viewers, and followers.

Some online journalism opportunities are found in large media markets such as New York City or Los Angeles, and at the nation's political center in Washington, DC. Other digital journalists work from communities of all sizes across the country, reporting for traditional mass media companies or for one of the growing number of online-only news outlets. These native digital news sources may target a niche audience with content focused on a specialized area of interest (such as Politico), or they may seek a broad general audience (like the Huffington Post). Using global connections via the information superhighway, an increasing number of journalists work from home or report "from the field." They can interview sources over the telephone or the Internet, conduct online research, and post articles directly to websites.

In general, journalists of all types work long hours and face demanding deadlines. Newspapers have daily deadlines, while a magazine may be completed each week or month. For online and broadcast journalists, however, deadlines appear instantly, as they must report the news in "real time" as it happens. Many journalists spend extra hours, weekends and holidays on the job, with the breaking news dictating their work schedule.

Digital journalists may report on a variety of topics for a large general interest news site, or they may focus on one particular area (such as sports, the environment, or political campaigns). Specializing in one segment makes the reporter more knowledgeable about the subject matter. Also, most small online outlets target a specific audience – such as sports fans or consumers with children. At these sites, journalists need to develop expertise in the niche subject their sites cover so they are at least as well informed as their readers.

Online news offers opportunities to write about a variety of important topics. The digital news universe has become far more comprehensive than simply passing along the latest celebrity scandal or tracking natural disasters. Some of these sites fill gaps that the larger media outlets overlook in local and national news. Others focus on investigative journalism, which mainstream media has largely abandoned because of its high expense. Many of the larger sites that support investigative journalism are run by nonprofit organizations, such as the Center for Public Integrity, ProPublica, and the Center for Investigative Reporting. Some of those nonprofits team up with established news organizations to help journalists uncover news that might otherwise be overlooked. Unlike print publications, online articles can be as long as is needed to tell the story, so digital investigative reports can run much longer than their traditional counterparts.

International news reporting is another area where native digital news sites have stepped into the void left as newspapers and television companies cut back on global reporting budgets. The Huffington Post has expanded from 11 to 15 countries. Vice Media, a news-streaming site, has 35 overseas bureaus, while BuzzFeed and Quartz have added coverage in Europe, Asia and Central America.

The demand for online news content is growing rapidly, with new sites being launched constantly, more traditional newsrooms expanding to the Internet, and consumers constantly seeking the latest news presented in an entertaining, informative fashion. One example comes from Pew Research, which notes that half of Facebook users get news through that social media site – even though they are not usually looking for news on Facebook. Half of the Internet users who watch videos online also view news videos on the web.

Another report by Reuter's news service finds that *The Atlantic* publishes as many articles online during one week as appear in its traditional monthly print magazine during the entire year. The report also notes that *The Atlantic* employs 50 digital journalists – significantly more than its print reporting staff.

The days of reporters hunched over typewriters in a noisy newsroom are long gone. Digital journalists use a variety of tools to do their jobs: computer laptops, email, blogging software, desktop publishing, graphic packages, social media feeds, and multimedia tools. Even those employed by traditional newspapers and magazines now work with a larger creative canvas than in the past. News articles from print publications are "repurposed" for online use. These reports may be edited into shorter, more search-engine friendly articles or blog posts. The news is also condensed into Twitter feeds and Facebook posts that "tease" readers to seek out the original article. Other sites may entirely reformat the article to add new graphics, video clips, audio for podcasts, and links to related online news articles. At some sites, digital journalists do many of these technical functions on their own. At others, they work with a team of creative technicians to add audio, visual and interactive elements to the basic news story.

Not all digital journalists perform as reporters or video editors. Some become content editors, a term that refers to preparing copy for online consumption. Editors do much more than simply check the facts and grammar in an article. They also mentor new hires and continually develop more experienced reporters. Some editorial positions are actually management positions that seldom require actual editing of copy. Editors may also fill roles that are more like the producers or directors found at a television network, working with journalists and technical resources to mold a multimedia presentation to tell news stories in unique, engaging ways.

At news aggregation sites, digital journalists often do not generate original content. Instead, they scour the Internet for news of interest to their readers. A site that focuses on the construction industry, for example, employs digital journalists to track down announcements, investigating reports, breaking news and analytical commentary that would interest professionals who work in the construction sector. Some rewrite the articles they find, perhaps better slanting that news to their target audience. They may simply collect hyperlinks to articles on other online sites and compile those into a single resource. Some news aggregation sites send out daily or weekly emails that summarize the news they find. Others rely on their subscribers (who may pay for the service) to come to the site whenever they wish, and find the news on their own schedule.

Most digital journalists are employees who work for one news outlet in return for a regular salary and benefits. However, many others are freelancers, self-employed journalists who contribute to multiple news sites and are paid for the content they create. While there are some freelancers who are able to make a living based solely on their digital journalism income, most also contribute to newspapers, magazines and other outlets as well as native news sites, to ensure a steady income. Many native news sites are not yet profitable, so the pay for freelancers often lags behind that from traditional media outlets.

DIGITAL JOURNALISTS TELL THEIR OWN STORIES

I Am a Native Digital Journalist

"When I was considering careers, journalism was not even on my list of priorities. For years I've enjoyed working with still photography and video. As a teenager, I wrote, photographed and edited my own movies, eventually posting clips to YouTube. So I thought I would end up at a movie or television studio, or as a magazine photographer.

However, while I was in high school, I was taking photos

for our school newspaper when I stumbled into digital journalism. Our teacher challenged us to take the articles and photos we put in our paper, and find new ways to expand those stories visually on the school website. I really enjoyed using words, pictures and sounds to bring our reports to life online and decided I wanted to become a digital journalist.

My portfolio of news stories, unpaid web posts, video blogs, and personal films helped me gain acceptance to Columbia University, home of the Tow Center for Digital Journalism. I learned to use a variety of visual and audio tools to convey news stories in ways that would engage the reader and keep them coming back for more. An internship with Mashable (one of the original native online news and aggregation sites) led to a full-time position there.

Now I spend my time gathering facts, shooting video and editing a finished product that allows me to communicate news to people around the world. I put together my own multimedia content, as well as help other journalists who do not have my strong video background. I'm having a great time helping Mashable pioneer new territory in the field of journalism, and can't wait to see where the digital revolution takes us next!"

I Am a Traditional Reporter Creating Online Content

"Like many journalists of my generation, I started my career as a newspaper reporter. Inspired by Bob Woodward and Carl Bernstein's reporting on the Watergate scandal in the 1970s, I wanted to become an investigative reporter cracking the big stories that made a difference, so I followed the traditional journalism career path. I graduated from the University of Georgia's Grady School of Journalism and Mass Communications. Then I landed an entry-level reporting job at a small paper in rural South Carolina, covering the city council and police beats, "chasing" fire trucks and ambulances on nights when there was local news to cover. I soon moved up to a larger paper in Charleston, and eventually to the *Atlanta Journal-Constitution* back home in Georgia.

My first 15 years in Atlanta were successful. I wrote about politics at the state capital, crisscrossed the state during the gubernatorial campaigns and built up a network of reliable sources to stay on top of the news. I didn't realize it at the time, but I got a lucky break in 2006. My editor wanted to post more timely news on our website during the statewide elections, so I learned about online reporting. In those days, we mainly took our print articles and posted them online without changes. Since I was among the first reporters at our paper to do this, I became the in-house expert as our publication moved more and more stories to the website.

Beginning in 2008, everything changed at the *Journal-Constitution,* and at other publications across the United States. For one thing, the global recession crushed the economy, and fewer advertisers meant less revenue for newspapers and magazines. At the same time, more people were getting their news online for free, so they stopped buying print publications. Free online classified ads also drew away income from the paper. For the next four years, our newsroom went through a series of downsizings, employee buyouts, and layoffs, as we tried to find a new model to compete, with fewer reporters and a tighter budget. Fortunately, my early experience with online reporting came in handy as we shifted resources to digital journalism.

By 2012, the resizing was over, but the newspaper business will never be the same again. I'm confident that digital journalism allowed me to keep my job while most of my colleagues departed. Now I'm an editor for the online news team, as well as writing features and investigative pieces. My focus is still on writing, but I have a great team of people around me who can find video clips or create interactive graphics that help us tell our stories in new ways I never dreamed of when I started 40 years ago. I'll be retiring soon, but I remain grateful I was here long enough to be part of the exciting transition to digital journalism."

PERSONAL QUALIFICATIONS

A CAREER IN DIGITAL JOURNALISM requires the traditional skills of an "old media" reporter, as well as the creative visual and technical skills to tell a story in the "new media" landscape.

For all journalists – digital included – writing is the most important part of the job. You must be able to express your ideas concisely, clearly and logically. Writing straight news copy is a skill you can pick up in journalism classes. You need to enjoy writing and revising stories if you are going to spend every day as a journalist.

Journalists also need to be curious, asking questions like "why" and "how" as they seek answers to questions arising from events they are covering. Reporters must be objective, providing impartial news accounts that present all views on a concern or incident. Journalists strive to keep their opinions out of their articles, presenting "just the facts" that enable readers to draw their own conclusions. They must guard against reporting inaccurate information that could subject their publication to lawsuits. Other helpful attributes include persistence, creative thinking, resourcefulness, and integrity. Good interpersonal skills are also required, when you are interviewing sources and creating on-location video reports.

Digital journalists require additional abilities in order to find new ways to tell stories in the online world. While some traditional reporters have transitioned into digital media, most editors and publishers are looking to hire younger journalists who have grown up in a web-enabled world. Newer reporters are accustomed to seeing visual content, and thus are often better equipped to create digital news that appeals to the younger viewers who comprise much of the online audience. Jim Roberts of news site *Mashable* told the Pew Research Center that he seeks new employees with a broader range of digital skills – "people who really understand visual journalism, and have an affinity for social media."

To tell a story well, digital journalists use video, graphics, audio clips, social media, and similar tools. Some advanced technical skills (such as film editing) can be learned in college and on the job, but the knack for telling stories visually comes from experience. It is acquired by being part of the audience – by using your laptop, smart phone or tablet to access news. For example, in online media, the news reporting style is more casual, personal and engaging than the more formal, dispassionate tone of newspapers, TV and radio. Traditional news is also limited by the type of media – a piece of paper, a time limited network broadcast – while digital news can include words, pictures, graphics, links to other articles, and all the other interactive attributes.

Digital journalists must be familiar with a variety of media platforms. They acquire and enhance their skills by using social media sites to communicate with friends, building their own websites, posting their own videos on YouTube, blogging about school news or current events, and using software for school projects. In some digital journalism engagements, you may be the technician working with a team of reporters, producers, graphic artists and videographers to create unique content for the world. While good writing techniques are always important, those skills are secondary to a knack for good storytelling. You will use a variety of digital tools to engage with your audience in innovative ways that get your message across with maximum impact.

ATTRACTIVE FEATURES

DIGITAL JOURNALISM CAN BE A highly rewarding and satisfying career. The online space offers vast opportunities for self-expression and creativity. "New" journalists entertain as well as inform their audiences, providing a valuable public service by sharing information with readers around the world. They are generally admired by the public and can become well-known celebrities.

If you like to be in the "middle of the action," a career in digital journalism will keep you on your toes. Reporters must stay on top of breaking news and current trends, aiming to be the first to tell their audiences about the latest developments. Depending on your beat, you may regularly interview sports stars, politicians, actors, celebrity chefs, or business executives. Your work may take you across the country or around the world to cover major events. You could be a travel journalist who visits and writes about an exclusive beach resort, or a critic reviewing a hip new downtown restaurant. You could become a blogger, shaping political opinions or entertaining your readers with humorous stories. Whatever area of interest you currently enjoy following in magazines, TV or websites is a category you could cover as a digital journalist.

Some digital journalists work in traditional newsrooms alongside conventional reporters and editors, while others are employed by native digital outlets that have an exclusive online presence. Those employed in one location work in clean, well-lit, modern publishing offices, broadcast studios, or technology centers. They have access to the latest state-of-the-art equipment and software to do their jobs. Digital journalists compose their stories on laptops, notebooks and tablet computers. They may also report directly from the scene of a news event through streaming video or satellite transmission, or record audio and video clips for digital editing back at the studio. Although journalism is generally a safe career with little risk of injury, those who cover wars and disasters may find themselves in physical danger.

Many digital journalists work from their homes, using the Internet to create content and to share it online. Some of these are staff writers for virtual publications, as many companies in the digital space have given up their brick-and-mortar offices for the convenience and lower costs of telecommuting. Other digital journalists are freelancers, self-employed professionals who work for a variety of publications. Freelancers generally run their own businesses and provide their own equipment, working from a dedicated space in their homes or reporting from the scene of breaking news stories.

Digital journalism is an exciting, promising new field that has only scratched the surface of creating engaging content on a variety of platforms. Many of these professionals are passionate about journalism – about digging out stories; editing content so it is easier to read; combining words, sounds and images to create an informative report; and telling fellow members of the community about what they need to know. Becoming a digital journalist can provide personal and professional satisfaction throughout your career.

UNATTRACTIVE ASPECTS

A DIGITAL JOURNALISM CAREER CAN BE demanding and stressful. Modern news is a 24/7 operation and the news cycles never end. Content creators often work long hours, nights and weekends to meet aggressive deadlines. Constant travel – such as following presidential candidates across the country as they seek votes and funds – can be exhausting over a long period of time. Even if you report for a local "hyper site," you may constantly crisscross your city or county, "chasing ambulances" to report on overnight accidents and crimes, or covering the high school football team's road games. News happens every day of the year, and digital journalists have to be available whenever and wherever news events occur. You might be fortunate enough to work on features where the pace is a little more relaxed, but feature journalists still have deadlines and production challenges.

While office conditions are generally good, journalists who work in a newsroom or other central location may find it difficult to concentrate. Writers, editors and technical staff generally share a common workspace with a number of other staffers. A newsroom can be a noisy and hectic environment, with digital content producers collaborating on pressing projects with tight deadlines. Digital reporters in traditional newsrooms are under added pressure to not write stories just for print publication. They must also constantly post and update stories on their papers' online sites, Twitter accounts, and other   platforms – even as the details of those stories are still developing.

Digital journalists in particular face constant demands for education to master existing technological platforms and learn the new ones that are being introduced at a tremendous pace. Those who follow a specific beat (such as technology) also have to understand that subject area and keep pace with new developments in the field. With the greater convergence of old and new media, even traditional newspaper reporters must be more knowledgeable about website layout, social media practices, videography and the other skills required to transform print articles into multimedia presentations. With tighter competition forecast, digital journalists find it is even more important to offer potential employers a broad range of storytelling skills to access the widest range of career options. More journalists are becoming self-employed freelancers, where they face the additional challenges of running a small business and constantly marketing themselves to find the next paying opportunity.

While few digital journalists face the risk of major injuries, some content providers (such as war correspondents or those covering natural disasters) may find themselves in physical danger. For all journalists, the long hours and constant deadline pressures can lead to health issues. Frequent computer use can bring eyestrain, back pain, and repetitive motion injuries such as carpal tunnel syndrome.

Many digital journalists work for smaller operations, where fewer workers mean they are expected to do everything – cover a number of beats, take their own photographs or videos, layout out their pages on websites, and constantly promote their articles through social media. Smaller shops often provide more diverse training opportunities than a large media center, but they can also pressure a new journalist to create more content, learn more skills and develop additional areas of expertise.

EDUCATION AND TRAINING

A BACHELOR'S DEGREE IN JOURNALISM, media, English, communications, or a similar discipline is generally required to get started. Video, audio and graphics are also an important part of digital journalism, so technical degrees in graphic design, multimedia development, website construction, or video production can also be helpful – particularly if you choose to focus on the technical environment. Some smaller online media outlets may accept a good writer with a high school diploma and a promising portfolio of work samples. However, many hiring editors require candidates to have a four-year degree and a solid portfolio of work samples.

Digital journalism requires a broader base of skills than those for traditional newspaper reporters. Still, the basic fundamentals of sound reporting and editing remain important at online publications. There are more than 1,500 colleges and universities that offer degrees in journalism and related fields. Of that number, the Accrediting Council in Journalism and Mass Communications (ACEJMC) accredits only about 100 programs in journalism and mass communications. Many of these schools offer degrees in digital communications, or at least some courses to help you navigate the evolving universe of online news.

Which undergraduate journalism program (usually referred to as J-school) is the best? Opinions vary among experts and rating systems, but several schools often come to the top of every list. For example, the recent survey by RTDNA (Radio Television Digital News Association) chose the University of Missouri School of Journalism as the top US J-school. Northwestern University was second, followed by:

University of Georgia

Syracuse University

Columbia University

Arizona State University-Walter Cronkite School

Ohio University

University of Florida

University of Montana

Lyndon State College/Electronic Journalism Arts

University of North Carolina

University of Maryland

Most of these same schools also have highly ranked journalism graduate schools. While a master's degree is not typically required to start your career, it can be helpful to advance your career, particularly if you plan to seek an editorial or management position. Columbia, Northwestern, Syracuse, Cal-Berkley and UNC-Chapel Hill are among those with leading graduate J-school programs.

While digital journalism is part of the curriculum at major J-schools, some programs have drawn specific attention for their focus on online career options. The industry website Journalism.com recently compiled this list of "five great digital journalism programs."

Columbia School of Journalism (Tow Center for Digital Journalism)

Virginia Polytechnic Institute and State University

University of Washington

San Francisco State University

California State University at Long Beach

When considering your educational options, start with national rankings of colleges and universities. There are general school rankings, such as those produced by US News and World Report each year, that include journalism school rankings. Also look for a copy of the current survey by Cox International Center at the University of Georgia. Cox conducts an annual survey of journalism and mass communications undergraduate and graduate programs across the country that includes valuable data.

After you narrow down your choices through research, visit the websites of potential schools to learn more details. Look for professors who have working experience as journalists, as those with real-world experience can best help you prepare for a working career. Pay particular attention to the availability of current technology so you can work with state-of-the-art hardware and software. Are there student online publications where you can contribute and grow your body of work? Are there internships available? Talk to the faculty to determine how closely the school matches your needs.

Take advantage of every opportunity to create work samples to add to your portfolio. Volunteer for both online and print outlets. The more versatility you demonstrate, the more value you offer to a future employer. Start a text or video blog. Build your own website. Write for your school newspaper, TV station, or online news outlets. Pursue internships that will provide demonstrable experience as a digital journalist. The more work samples you can accumulate, the better positioned you will be to get that critical first job after graduation. Plus, the more news pieces you create, the better journalist you become. Actively seek out mentors, such as professors and working journalists.

Your education does not end when you become employed. State press associations can provide training on such topics as libel laws. The Reynolds Center for Business Journalism offers free online and in-person training to help reporters cover business news more effectively. The Society for Professional Journalists focuses on issues around press rights, open records laws, and using the Freedom of Information Act to access federal government information.

Digital journalism will continue evolving for the foreseeable future, and opportunities will arise in unanticipated places. The more skills you can learn – from video blogging to social media – the more career options you will have. The need to keep learning and growing is particularly keen in these highly competitive careers. No matter how good a writer you may be, there is always room for improvement through continual practice. And no matter how good a journalist you become, there is always a new interviewing technique to learn, new technology to master and new media outlets to consider.

EARNINGS

SALARIES FOR NEWS ANALYSTS, REPORTERS, correspondents and editors vary widely across different journalism platforms. Median annual wages of reporters and correspondents in all types of employment are about $45,000, according to the most recent studies, while median wages of broadcast news analysts are over $55,000. Editors earn about $60,000.

Digital journalists are classified in several different ways in studies of average earnings.

Graphic designers
$45,000

Photographers
$35,000

Film and video editors and camera operators
$50,000

Online media editors
$65,000

Digital reporters and correspondents
$55,000

Visual journalists working in streaming video
$55,000

From another viewpoint, the Pew Research Center found there are more than 5,000 digital journalists working at native news sites.

The pay range can be even wider for digital journalists than for traditional journalists. According to SimplyHired.com, the average salary for a digital journalist is about $50,000. The jobs are multimedia journalists, content writers, interactive digital creators, producers, and interactive graphics journalists. While some companies pay rates that are competitive with traditional news outlets, others pay lower salaries for online journalists because online sites generate less revenue.

Media outlets have experimented with various formulas tying compensation to a journalist's ability to bring in an audience, such as pay-per-page-view and pay-per--unique-web-visitor. Another model implemented recently by the Toronto Star newspaper in Canada is to pay newly-hired digital journalists less than other staff in the same newsroom. A newspaper spokesperson said print revenues are nine times greater than online income, so the publication would pay digital writers about $850 a week versus $1,000 for entry-level reporters.

OPPORTUNITIES

THE CAREER OUTLOOK FOR DIGITAL JOURNALISTS is more promising than for traditional journalists. While print publications are expected to continue declining in popularity, growth is predicted to continue at online-only content sources and in the web-based operations of traditional media outlets. Competition will remain high for the available jobs in traditional media (newspapers, magazines, television and radio), as companies expand opportunities in online media. Web-based content is attracting both newcomers with advanced technical skills, as well as veteran reporters and editors transitioning into new media.

Overall, employment of reporters, correspondents and broadcast news analysts is expected to decline by about 10 percent. Declining revenues at traditional media outlets will negatively impact employment growth.

 Although the total number of jobs for reporters is expected to drop from about 55,000 to 50,000, digital journalism opportunities at traditional media outlets will continue to rise. There will be increased demand for online news and podcasts. As a result of these trends, reporters, correspondents and broadcast news analysts face increased competition for fewer positions – although candidates with digital journalism skills have an advantage. Multimedia journalism experience, including video photography and editing skills will definitely improve your career opportunities. With newspapers and TV stations publishing more and more content on multiple media platforms, employers will favor applicants who have experience in website design.

The exact number of digital journalists currently working is unclear. Government analysts estimate there are over

200,000 people in all information services – a classification that includes news syndicates, exclusive Internet publishing and broadcasting, web search portals, digital libraries, and archives. Editors make up the largest occupation in the sector with over 6,000 employed.

The Pew Research Journalism Project estimates there are some 5,000 editorial-related jobs in the digital news sector. Pew breaks the digital news space into two parts: the hundreds of outlets with a small number of employees, and the 30 largest digital media outlets. The larger outlets account for more than 3,000 jobs, while some 450-plus small sites account for about 2,000 positions.

Meanwhile, a survey by the University of Georgia indicates that the job market for journalists overall is rebounding from the post-recession years. The study found over two-thirds of journalism graduates today start a full-time job within eight months of graduation, versus only about 50 percent in recent years. The study also found online journalists are drawing larger salaries, while the pay for magazine and radio reporters is lagging below industry averages.

GETTING STARTED

ARE YOU READY TO PURSUE A CAREER AS a digital journalist? Choosing your future profession is an important first step, but do not stop there. There are many other steps you can take now to start preparing for the future.

Begin by gathering more detailed information about the many career paths for digital journalists. Then think about how you can begin working towards your goal. Print and online information about communications careers is widely available at libraries, from colleges and universities, and through your school's guidance counselors. The Internet is a vital resource – and not just because of current examples of digital journalism. It also provides a broad range of easily accessible data from media companies, government agencies, professional associations, and recruiters who help candidates find employment. Include in your research traditional media outlets, including newspapers, magazines and broadcasters. They also employ digital content creators, and their websites may mention qualifications for their job openings.

Before you start college, look for ways to get experience as a journalist. Volunteer for your school paper, start a blog, build your own or contribute items to locally-oriented news sites like Patch or Examiner. There are many other websites that accept columns and articles from writers with no prior experience (typically for little or no pay). Actively seek out internship opportunities with local media outlets. Any article that appears in print or on line will add to your collection of "clips" and build up your portfolio as you progress from high school to college, and eventually into the work force.

Plus, it is never too early to start taking classes to learn your new trade. There are online and "live" courses that will help – not just on becoming a journalist, but also to develop photography, blogging, multimedia storytelling, digital video, social media and similar skills that are highly prized by employers.

You will need a four-year degree in journalism or communications to get started, so check out which colleges and universities can provide the contemporary digital training you need. Also think about how you will get some preliminary experience to help land that first job. Are there internships or volunteer opportunities available near the school you are considering? You may be able to find a part-time, entry-level position that will enhance your résumé and provide some extra money.

Seek out people who work as digital journalists, or other professionals who work closely with these journalists (such as editors and videographers). Ask what skills will help applicants find a position and advance in their careers.

You can find knowledgeable individuals through professional associations or local publications. Industry associations can help you learn about the local market. They are also a great source for leads on scholarships, internships, and vocational training programs. Most states and metropolitan areas have active press associations that include digital journalists. Many of these groups have outreach programs targeting potential and current journalism students. Some others let students join and attend sessions at a lower cost than the general public.

Call upon your personal network for support and advice. Discuss your plans with family and friends. Do they think digital journalism would be a good fit for your personal strengths and interests? Talk over your plans with your school counselor, who can share helpful information about local educational opportunities, employment prospects, and networking venues.

Once you gather your data, it is time to give careful thought to whether a career as a digital journalist feels right for you. Are you comfortable with the educational requirements? Can you write quickly, concisely and accurately? Do you like experimenting and mastering technology – particularly video and social media? Would you be content working long hours to cover breaking news? Do you work well under pressure?

The most important consideration is whether you can see yourself enjoying a successful career as a digital journalist. If it seems like the right choice for you, start taking those first steps today towards a rewarding, fulfilling career!

ASSOCIATIONS

■ **American Society of Journalists and Authors**
http://www.asja.org

■ **Association of Young Journalists and Writers**
http://www.ayjw.org

■ **Council of National Journalism Associations**
www.journalismassociations.com

■ **International Press Association**
http://internationalpress.com

■ **Investigative Reporters and Editors**
http://www.ire.org

■ **JEA (Journalism Education Association)**
http://jea.org

■ **JEA Digital Media Resource**
http://www.jeadigitalmedia.org

■ **National Federation of Press Women**
http://www.nfpw.org

■ **National Freedom of Information Coalition**
http://www.nfoic.org

■ **National Press Club**
http://press.org

■ **National Press Foundation**
http://nationalpress.org

■ **Online News Association**
http://journalists.org

- Reporters Association for Freedom of the Press
http://www.rcfp.org

- Society of Environmental Journalists
http://www.sejarchive.org/pub
/index.htm

- Society of Professional Journalists
http://www.spj.org

- University Film & Video Association
http://www.ufva.org

PERIODICALS

- American Journalism Review
http://www.ajr.org

- American Press Institute
http://www.naafoundation.org

- Columbia Journalism Review
http://www.cjr.org

- Current
http://www.current.org

- Editor and Publisher
http://www.editorandpublisher.com

- eJournalist
http://www.ejournalist.au

- Folio
http://www.foliomag.com

- Huffington Post
www.huffingtonpost.com

■ **Online Journalism Review**
http://www.ojr.org

■ **Video Maker Magazine**
http://www.videomaker.com

■ **Wikinews**
http://en.wikinews.org

■ **Writers Digest**
http://www.writersdigest.com

■ **Writers' Journal**
http://www.writersjournal.com

WEBSITES

■ **Associated Press**
http://www.ap.org

■ **Copyediting**
http://www.copyediting.com

■ **HARO (Help A Reporter Out)**
http://www.helpareporter.com

■ **Journalism Jobs**
http://www.journalismjobs.com

■ **Intern Match**
http://www.internmatch.com

■ **Introduction to Film Editing**
http://www.introtoediting.com

■ **Magazine Journalism Internships**
http://www.internships.com/intern/journalism
/magazine

■ **Media Bistro**
http://www.mediabistro.com

■ Pew Research Center for People and the Press
http://www.people-press.org

■ Poynter Center for Media Studies
http://www.poynter.org

■ Reynolds Center for Business Journalism
http://businessjournalism.org

■ The Pulitzer Prizes
http://www.pulitzer.org

■ Writers Weekly
http://www.writersweekly.com